A STILLNESS without SHADOWS

Joseph J. Juknialis

Resource Publications Inc.
160 E. Virginia St. Suite 290
San Jose, CA 95112

Editorial Director: Kenneth Guentert
Production Editor: Scott Alkire
Inside Design: Christine Benjamin
Inside Illustrations: Mark Helmich
Mechanical Layout: Geoff Rogers, Ron Niewald

ISBN 0-89390-081-8
Library of Congress Catalog Number: 86-62620
Printed and Bound in the United States 5 4 3 2

TABLE
of
CONTENTS

a STILLNESS without SHADOWS

GOLDEN APPLES

Throughout the entire village the children were wrapped in excitement, for it was the eve of the Feast of St. Nicholas, the night the saint himself made a visit to every home. To every child he came, bringing fruits and nuts and sometimes a trinket or a toy and then stuffing those gifts into drooping stockings hung on the front door of every home.

To some homes he came near supper time. To others he came much later, as everyone was ready for bed. And still to others he came later in the night or early morning while it was still dark and everyone slept. Quietly and unnoticed, he would fill the socks and then announce his visit with a wrap so loud that it brought everyone rushing to the door. Always, of course, the visiting saint would have disappeared by the time the door was opened.

Of all the gifts he gave, the most desired was a shiny red apple, and the most feared was a sock full of coal. The apple, as it happened, had become a symbol that the boy or girl who owned the sock had been good and well behaved. Over the years, however, the apple had taken on another meaning as well — that Christmas would bring the longed-for gifts. Coal, of course, became the mark of Cain and the sign of a giftless Christmas.

Now it should be known that while every child in the village dreaded the possibility of a stocking full of coal, no one ever received anything but a shiny red apple. Yet each year older brothers and sisters would tell stories of someone who had gotten only coal on the eve of St. Nicholas' feast, and, as a result, nothing — not even coal — on Christmas itself.

For days now, the children had grown restless and eager. The oldest and baggiest socks had been pulled and stretched even further. Threats of coal had been leveled against the mischievous. Chores were being finished without even reminders. Finally, the long awaited night came, and darkness covered the village with quiet excitement.

The first home visited was on the edge of the village, along the mountain creek which ribboned the forest. All in that family had settled down around the fireplace, playing games beside the friendliness of the fire. It was shortly after supper and all the dishes had been washed. Suddenly, a pounding on the door caught the family off guard. Together, everyone scurried to the door and swung it open. Of course, St. Nicholas had come and gone — unseen — but the stockings on the door now hung stuffed and stretched and bulging with gifts. The children jumped and shouted and reached up to lift each stocking off the nail which held it. They rushed to the living room and knelt on the floor in the light of the fire, spilling their treasures into the warmth.

Then, one at a time, each child grew silent and embarrassed. Each had found coal. No one received a shiny red apple. They looked at one another and saw that each had been treated the same. Questions mingled with their tears. Why? What had they done wrong? Would Christmas now be empty? Though their parents hugged them and tried to explain that there must have been a mistake or someone's bad joke, nothing seemed to ease the pain. What would they tell their friends? How would they explain the coal when everyone else brought a shiny red apple to school?

Little did they know that on that night the very same scene took place in every home in the village. On that St. Nicholas' Eve, no one received a red apple. Everyone had found coal in their stocking on the door.

The next day, sadness filled the seats of the desks in the school. At first, no one told of the coal he or she had received. Then, one by one, they realized no one had a red apple to show. Finally, one young girl found the courage to say that she had found coal in the stocking on her door. From across the room another girl stood and told the same story. A boy followed — and then another child and another — until everyone revealed that they and all in their family had found coal in their stockings, and that no one had received that longed for sign of goodness and favor — the shiny red apple.

When the people of the village realized what had taken place, they were stunned. No one understood. No one could explain. Day by day they grew more and more quiet, more and more withdrawn. If no one had received a shiny red apple, they concluded, then there was no one in the village worthy of being loved or capable of loving in return. Then there was no goodness, only selfishness and much darkness. As the days of Christmas grew closer, the joy and happiness which should have come with those days grew more and more distant.

In all the village only one person knew what had taken place and why it was that no one received an apple, but rather only coal. That one person was an old lady who lived on the backside of the village and in the shadows of everyone else's busyness. She had spent her entire life in the village, and in fact, was the oldest of all its inhabitants. Over the years, there had been much pain in her life, and one by one she closed the windows and doors of her world until no one even knew her name. Everyone simply called her "the old lady."

Mara was her name, however, and she had grown so lonely and so in need of love that her spirit yearned for any bit of favor or acceptance. It had been years since she had received a shiny red apple on the eve of St. Nicholas' feast, or even any coal. It seemed that she, who lived in the shadows, had been overlooked by everyone, even by the one who was the bearer of apples.

In her quiet desperation, Mara decided that this year she, too, would delight in an apple. On the edge of the village, and in the darkness of that night, the old lady waited for the bearer of apples. Her intention was simply to ask for an apple when she saw the saint arrive. Yet when the hooded figure in flowing robes with a shepherd staff did come, she became frightened and ashamed. Instead, she followed him from house to house. As he left one home and moved on to the next, she began grasping the apples he left in the stockings on the doors. As she did so, she reached for handfuls of the coal which every yard held, and she stuffed the coal into the places from where she had taken the apples. All this she did quickly, before the door was opened by those eagerly awaiting the saint's rap.

Much later she wondered why she had taken so many apples, and why she had followed the saint throughout the village, taking for herself every apple he left. Strangely enough, though the old lady now had many apples, each a symbol of goodness and love, she still felt lonely and forgotten.

In the days immediately before Christmas, Mara grew to realize the impact of what she had brought about. She began to sense the joylessness of those days which, in years past, had overflowed with song and cheer. Bit by bit she understood, in a way she never had before, the power of the shiny red apple and what it held for each person in the village. Finally, Mara decided that she, who had brought about the dreary gloom, also needed to be the one that would restore the joy.

As Christmas eve approached, the villagers made their way to the church just as they had always done. But this year it was different. They came sadly and in silence. If, they had come to believe, there was no love among them, how could they celebrate the birth of the one who is love?

On the stroke of midnight, the churchbells rang and the organ played and the choir sang. Candles were lighted and filled the darkness. Everyone smiled politely and wished a "Merry Christmas" to their neighbors. Yet the spirit which gives life to Christmas was not present.

Outside, the old lady who had filled her sack with shiny red apples weeks before, now stood listening and watching. Satisfied that she was alone, she went quickly to the large evergreen growing in the village square in front of the church. While everyone prayed, she quickly hung the newly polished apples on the tree. With a long pole, she carefully placed the apples on those branches too high for her to reach. Slowly the tree came alive. Each apple, as it caught the moonlight bouncing off the new snow, grew brighter and brighter. Each apple glowed with moonlight and grew so brilliant that it seemed to have become a golden apple.

Just as Mara finished hanging the last apple, the final carol was played. The church doors opened, and the villagers came forth. Everyone stood in awe as they gazed upon the tree bedecked with golden apples. The children shouted and screamed with excitement while their parents looked on in amazement. Someone rushed into the church and the bells began to ring again. Carols were sung, over and over. Neighbors wished "Merry Christmas" as if it were the first

time, and the children danced around the tree. It was indeed Christmas. The villagers now knew they were loved after all for they had been blessed with golden apples.

Finally, after much singing and dancing, the youngest began to grow tired and sleepy. Wearily, they found their way to the restful arms of their mothers and fathers. Before long, one family after another began to leave for their Christmas homes, but not before they stopped at the tree, each to take home with them a golden apple, a symbol of their love and goodness.

Mara watched all this from the shadows of the village square — from those very shadows which were home for her throughout most of every year. She watched not in sadness now, but with a very silent joy, knowing that every family had found, in a way never before known, that it was indeed filled with goodness and love. After everyone had gone, after the church had been locked and the square had been tucked in silence for the remainder of that night, the old lady slowly made her way back to the tree. She smiled to herself, feeling good about the love she had been party to bringing. It was, indeed, a most holy Christmas, she thought. The best.

One last time Mara walked around the tree, remembering the dancing and the happiness which had surrounded it a short time before. She was about to leave for home when her eye caught a glimmer. She looked again, and there on the tree was one, lone golden apple. How strange, she thought, that there was one extra, one more than those she had gathered from all the stockings a few weeks before. Yet there it hung, golden and brilliant. She looked around. Everyone had left. She alone remained in the square. And so, Mara reached up and picked the golden apple. In that moment, her heart danced. She, too, was loved. She, too, had an apple. Tears slipped down her cheeks as she glowed within, more brilliantly than the apple she held in her hands. As Mara made her way home that early Christmas morning, she thought to herself that it was, without exception, a most loving Christmas, not only because she too had received a golden apple, but because she also realized her love for everyone in the village.

After Mara had left and made her way into that holy night, the square remained quiet. The only sound came from the Christmas wind, and in the shadows of the church a hooded figure, in flowing robes with a shepherd staff, smiled to himself, and then silently disappeared.

BREAD
THAT
REMEMBERS

A long time ago
people had not yet forgotten
that bread always remembers
what is spoken in its presence.
Then everyone knew that if goodness was spoken
among those gathered around the bread
then those who ate that bread would be blessed;
and if it was selfishness and evil that was spoken
why then those who ate the bread would be cursed
with cold hearts and hardened spirits.

There were in those days two brothers.
Many thought them to be twins
for they looked so much alike
not only in appearance
but also in what they did
and how they treated others.
However, though they were born in the same year,
they were not twins,
for the older had been born in January
and the younger in December of that very same calendar.
Their mother had died in giving birth to the younger,
and so the two brothers

9

had been raised by their kind and loving father —
each reflecting his goodness and gentleness.
Perhaps that is why they were thought to be twins
by the many who knew them.

One day in early spring,
after they had grown to young manhood,
yet before either of them had married and left home,
their father grew seriously ill.
Before the seeds of that season had sprouted with life
the father died,
leaving his sons, then, to depend upon their own goodness.

Together the two brothers came before the judge of that land
so that the father's will might be unsealed
in order that each might receive
what the father had promised.
The reading of that will
revealed equal portions of life for each of the sons.
Because the father had loved them both,
without favoritism of any sort,
each of the sons received half of the farm
on which he had been raised.

At this, the elder son grew angry and resentful.
He had deserved the greater share, he insisted,
for he was the older of the two;
and with that he turned away from the judge
and from his brother
and left them both
alone
in that chamber of justice.

When the older brother arrived home
he sat in anger
at the very table where he and his brother
together with their father
had shared meals
and love
and life.
There, at that table,
he allowed his anger to unravel more and more.

10

Shattering the gentle stillness which had long been a family member,
he spewed curses and hatred
at the embarrassed and lonely silence.
Suddenly
he stood,
pounded the table with yet more violence,
and left.
In all of his anger
what the elder brother had never noticed
was the bread on the table.

Shortly thereafter the younger brother came home.
Having found the elder brother gone,
he sat and waited amid the stained silence.
When the older brother never returned
the younger brother ate his evening meal alone
in the torn darkness of that night.
There he ate the bread which had heard the elder's anger,
the bread that remembered.
That night the heart of the younger brother
grew cold and hardened,
scarred with the same selfishness and hatred
which lived within the elder.

The next day's morning sun
was the sole source of light in the brothers' home.
The older brother did return
but without the gentleness and love which once were his.
So also did the younger brother live
without his father's gifts,
twinned again,
though now in hatred
as once they had been in goodness and peace.

During those weeks of summer,
the entire countryside came to recognize the change
which had come about between the two brothers.
Their hearts quietly wept in sadness
over that tragic occurrence.

Somewhere in the middle of that summer
the wise one of the village

invited the inhabitants of the surrounding countryside
to a common meeting.
On a warm summer evening
all but the two brothers
came to the village square in the center of the town.
Men and women gathered;
children tagged along;
strangers were welcomed.

There, on the table in the center of their gathering,
was placed a single loaf of bread.
When it seemed that all had arrived,
the one who was wise came before them
and explained why he had called them together.
If it is true that the bread always remembers, he said,
then perhaps we can bring blessings of gentleness and love
once again.
He then invited all those who had come
to tell stories of the goodness
which once lived in the hearts
of both the elder and the younger brother,
and to tell those stories in the presence of the bread —
the bread that always remembers.

One by one, then, they came forward
and stood before the bread
and before their neighbors,
there to tell their own story
of how they had been blessed with life
by the two brothers.

Many stories were told that night,
all in the presence of the bread.
There were stories of how the two had once
taken in a stranger who was sick and lost,
and other stories of the time a neighbor had broken a leg
at the beginning of the planting season
and how the brothers worked nights
by moonlight
to plant his fields
after they had planted their own

in order that the neighbor might have crops to harvest
come autumn.
Others told stories of how the brothers
had shared half of their own harvest with a neighbor
when his barn burned
and, with the barn, all of that season's labors as well.

All evening long villagers and countryfolk
stood in front of everyone
and, in the presence of that lone loaf of bread,
told stories of the gentleness and goodness
which once had made a home among the brothers.
When the last story had been told,
well past the time when many of the children had fallen asleep
in the arms of their parents,
all those who had gathered
made their way to their homes
and to the healing sleep which awaited them.

After all had left
the wise one who had gathered them all
stood alone at the table with the bread.
There, in the summer silence of that night,
he picked up the loaf of bread,
placed it in a sack,
and began his journey to the home of the two brothers.
He arrived just before the sun,
when the nighttime had not yet begun to shed
her skin of darkness.
His deed was simple
and quickly done —
to leave the bag which held the bread at the door
and depart.

As he made his way home
amid the early showers of morning sun,
he realized he was not tired
though he had not slept the entire night.
Instead, he felt within himself
a rising hope of life,
fed by the faint possibility

that perhaps the two brothers,
when they found the bread,
might just offer each other that bread
and with it
all of the goodness and gentleness and love
it remembered.

THE
GOLDEN
DOVE

If you listen to the wind and to the tales she tells, you will hear of how the dove flew from the ark and out among the first signs of new life. Mountain peaks newly brushed with green, and ribbons of rushing mountain streams, and bold cliffs of majestic stone seemed scattered everywhere. Filled with excitement, the dove flew straight to God, simply to say thank you for all the new life. God was so pleased with the dove's gratitude and thoughtfulness that he breathed his spirit of peace into the dove; and when God did so, the dove took on a golden brilliance. From that moment on, even until today, stories have been told that once in every century the golden dove of peace appeared wherever it found peace dwelling in abundance — but only once in every century.

One such story tells of an old man and woman, grown weary and weak by the burden of their years. Together they simply waited for God's final coming into their lives. One winter night, when the cold was bitter and the wind bold, they heard a knock upon their door. Though fearful of the harm that might come upon them in their old age, they opened the door of their simple home. There a stranger, cold and hungry, stood in the doorway, as if suspended between winter's hell and the heaven within. Without hesitation, the couple invited the stranger into their home, then fed him and offered him their

17

own bed. That night the old husband and wife slept on the hard floor in front of the fire which slowly died in the course of the night. When morning came, the couple awoke to find the stranger had risen and gone. The bed was empty, except for a golden dove which nested upon the pillow.

There is yet another tale of three wise men who came to visit the new born child Jesus. They came bringing gifts, it is told — gifts of gold and frankincense and myrrh. Legend has it that the gold they brought was in the form of a dove — indeed, a golden dove of peace for the one who is peace.

Still another story tells of the time when two young girls grew up together and went to the same school. Because of some silly argument, they vowed never to speak to one another again. Though they continued to live in the same town, they never did speak, even as they were both well on in years. Then after years of silence, one woman had a change of heart, and in her sorrow she baked a loaf of bread and placed it in a sack in front of the door of the other. When the other opened her door, and then the sack which held the bread, out of the sack flew a golden dove.

Such are only a few of the many tales told from one generation to the next about the golden dove of peace and how that dove has appeared once in every century. What follows here is the tale of the last time the golden dove appeared, well over a hundred years ago. Know well, then, that the golden dove has not yet appeared in this century of ours!

The story is told that, far from our land and far across the sea among a distant people, a vicious army was making its way across that land, devouring both farm and village on its way. The dream of the one who led the army was to someday rule the entire world. So, with much greed and little mercy, his army moved relentlessly forward.

A tiny village heard of the advancing army when it was yet a long way off. The citizens decided they would resist, and they began to make weapons for themselves. They shaped spears and swords, hammered shields, and cast cannons and guns as well. The villagers hid their tools of violence, strangely, in the basement of the village church. There the arsenal grew day by day, turning a harbor of peace into a haven of destruction.

What no one knew, however, was that while everyone in the village built weapons for defense, a young girl each day slipped away into the steeple of the church. There, high above the townsfolk, she began to make paper doves — enough so that she might give one to each of the soldiers in the invading army — then perhaps she might persuade them toward peace.

Each day brought stories of approaching terror and was marked with an ever-increasing number of weapons. Each day, as well, dawned upon more and more paper doves. First, one hundred seemed a monstrous task, but the young girl's fingers grew skilled and nimble, and soon there were five hundred and then eight hundred paper doves.

Finally, the dreaded day arrived when the invading army entered the village. The villagers huddled in the basement of their church, fearful in the midst of hoaned steel and violence, while the young girl sat high above them, perched in the steeple of that same church and quietly at peace amid a thousand paper doves.

Upon entering the village, the army found only silence. The soldiers quickly searched the homes and shops, yet they found no one. Eventually, they positioned themselves in the square opposite the church. Both the villagers within and the army without waited for opening doors to signal the battle. It was the leader of the army, then, who approached the church and, with one swift motion, swung wide the doors.

Suddenly, out through the doors of the church flew a thousand white doves of peace. They flew like a cresting wave; higher and higher the flock circled the village square. Around and around and around they flew, all morning long. The army stood at one side of the square and the villagers on the other, face to face in front of the church, while the thousand white doves of peace flew around above them. All knew that as long as the doves would fly, no one would dare do battle. All morning long the doves flew. Noon came and passed and still they flew. All afternoon the flight went on. The thousand white doves circled the square again and again, imprisoning in peace the violence below. Slowly everyone realized that once the nighttime darkness came and hid the circling doves and once they could be seen no more, then the enemies in the square would do battle.

In late afternoon, the sun began to set in the western sky, and all in the square watched as the horizon stole the last day of peace. Then, as if out of the sun, a lone dove flew toward the village. To all those gathered there, the dove seemed to be the color of the sun, shining

19

and brilliant. Closer and closer came that dove, until it was close enough for all to see that it was indeed a golden dove. It flew directly to the center of the square, and there it landed. Everyone stood amazed, and all marveled at how they had been blessed, for the golden dove of peace had come once again, this time in their century. Then, all the villagers and all the soldiers lay down their weapons. No more could they do violence or bear arms. No more could they find glory in battle or in victory.

In the face of peace, the leader of the army grew furious. He could not allow a simple winged creature to ruin his dream of world conquest. Lest his dream die there, the leader boldly stepped out into the center of the square. Then he drew his saber, and before anyone could realize what he was about to do, he cut out the heart of the golden dove of peace. The people gasped, then screamed and cried; but the leader was not to be overcome. He was determined to have his dream fulfilled.

Suddenly, the golden dove began to fly. Higher and higher it flew, toward the thousand doves circling above. And all below realized that as long as peace lived in their own hearts, they would give life and be the heart of the golden dove. There would indeed be peace.

The golden dove flew higher and higher and was surrounded by the thousand circling white doves, until all of them appeared to be a huge white sphere in the sky with the golden dove as its center. As those below gazed on, darkness came upon the land, but everyone knew without a doubt that peace would reign.

That night, the villagers invited the soldiers into their homes. They fed them and cared for them and offered them their beds. Outside, in the village square, one lone figure sat in the darkness. Only he, the leader of the invading army, could not understand what had taken place. For all the others, villagers and soldiers alike, peace had come. Into their lives, the golden dove of peace had flown and life now beat with a new heart.

21

M HELLMICH

THE
CUP

I

It was a winter sewn with the thread of pain, sewn to a tattered autumn at one end and to an as yet unshrunk spring on the other — a winter which lingered too long, so that the gray of the clouds cast musty shadows on everyone's spirit.

That winter created David in its own image — in the image of shunned loneliness. Like stale snow which took too long to melt, David urgently longed for the next season of life. Unfortunately, that year spring dallied.

David lived life adolescently alone, suspended like a morning star between nighttime and daytime, between parents and peers, between the wishfulness of childhood and the wistfulness of adulthood.

23

David remembered years past, when he had been a child, and his parents had spoken of Athena, a woman old and wise, who lived in the hills. She could uncover the meaning in life, were it to be sought, they said. It was she who could heal, if lives or hearts were torn open. Most important to David at this time, it was this woman who could give direction to life when those who lived it seemed lost. It was to seek this direction that David set out one day in search of Athena.

To David it seemed the hills had a guiding spirit all their own. Though he began the journey without knowing the course, in their own magic-touched way the hills nudged him and led him deeper and deeper into what David hoped was the realm of Athena's wisdom. What David did not know was that it was also the beginning of an ever deepening journey into his own future.

Sometime during the afternoon of that first day of his journey, he grew weary. Though he had always been strong as a youth, his energy now seemed borrowed and ill-fitting as if it were not his own. Though he had always been keen of mind and astute to his surroundings, everything now seemed diluted. Strangest of all, he felt not alone. He sat respectfully on the wintered earth and leaned back against the trunk of an old tree. With his head bowed forward and his chin sewn to his chest, David was stolen into the realm of the one who is wise.

A warm gentle breeze then parted David's sleep. He was not sure if he now lived a dream unfolded to appear more clear, or if he dreamed a life dusted with a touch of fantasy. Whichever, the wisdom David sought now stood in front of him. There was no need to ask who this woman was. David knew. More than the silver hair which framed her face and draped her shoulders, more than the simply woven gown loosely tied at the waist with a woven vine — more than either of these, it was the eyes which lifted David's heart and told him he had come upon Athena who is wise.

"You are David," said Athena, "and you come in search of me. Is that not so?" David agreed with only a nod. To have done more would somehow have made the moment less holy, it seemed. "You come because you seek a focus for your life, a meaning, perhaps most of all a direction. You find yourself amid people, yet you are lonely. You live in a world which insists that its truths give life, yet you grow more empty. Now you have come here in your youth, hoping to find an answer. Your spirit bears the unbridled enthusiasm of youth, yet your heart seeks the patient wisdom of age. I must tell you now, David, it cannot be — both dwelling in one soul. But do not be saddened. To know that much is already to have begun the journey, for one unfolds into the other much as a storming stream seeks the sea, much as a shattered seed in time bears fruit. You shall be wise, I promise, but your journey must first make its own way to wisdom."

Then Athena, the one who is wise, held out to David a cup. "From the cup, David, you must drink whenever the way seems unsure. It holds a promise. Trust in that promise and you will learn the meaning of your call, the thrust of your vocation. It is there if you only look."

Suddenly the gentle breeze turned harsh. The warmth withdrew. The youth who had come searching lifted his head to look again into the hills which cradled him. He had come seeking the one who is wise, and thought it strange to have found her in a dream. Yet, David wondered, was it only that — a dream and no more? He asked himself if he should continue. Dreams, he had always thought, were born more of wish than of life. Yet the dream had asked him to trust in the promise of the cup — whatever that promise would show itself to be. Already he found himself hesitant and unfaithful. David was confused. If only the tree which had stood guard as he dreamt could tell the tale of those brief moments, David mused, then he would know what it was he should do.

Still unsure, he stood up. About to seek a place to spend the night, he noticed beside him the cup held out to him by Athena in the dream. Suddenly, it was all real. David's heart shouted. He had been given a promise, a meaning for his life. He would come to know it, he now knew, and when he was unsure, he would drink from the cup. David rejoiced. He had journeyed into the hills and had found not only the one who is wise but also all which he hoped for from her.

That year it snowed no more. Winter had given way to spring. David was no longer a child. The seed had been shattered and had sprouted, yet it would be many seasons before fruit would be borne.

II

During the next few years, David continued to live at home. In that time he never once shared the events of the day spent journeying into the hills. No one ever knew of Athena whom he had met nor of the cup he had been given.

Eventually David began to sense that he was being led by the spirit within him to make his own way in life. He explained that to his family, gathered all he owned, and spoke his goodbyes. He took with him the cup he had been given. Though he had quickly hidden it when he had returned home from the hills, the memory of it had not been hidden. So it was that David and the cup began their journey.

For almost two years David wandered among the villages and lives and stories scattered over the land. People were always kind, yet so often he felt lonely. His days were not greatly different than those before he had met Athena. It was a matter of spirits — his and theirs — neither ever finding a home in the other. In all this time, David never once drank from the cup he had been given long before. To him, it seemed the time had not yet come. He would know when, he always felt.

One day David came upon a village he had not yet seen. When David smiled, the villagers smiled, and quickly they became friends. When David shared what little he had, the villagers did likewise and opened their homes to him. David's own spirit so trusted the goodness he had found that before long, he told the villagers what he had never told any other — the story of his journey into the hills and how he had met Athena and her wisdom. Yet of the cup, David never spoke. That much, he had decided, he would keep to himself.

Before long, David decided he would stay among the villagers and make their home his home. They were delighted with David's decision for in so many ways their spirits had become one. During all this time, David had saved what earnings he made, and soon he was able to make a payment toward the purchase of a small home on a tiny parcel of land just outside the village. There he could find silence for his spirit yet be near the family his heart had found. And always David wondered if the time would ever come to drink from the cup he had been given. To him, it seemed, there would never be a need.

One evening, shortly after the sun had given the moon charge over the land, a knock came at David's door. He went to open the door, and found a stranger, much older than himself and weary looking, with a sadness in his eyes. David smiled a welcome, and with that the stranger smiled back, relieved that the night could be so kind as to offer a friendly face. The stranger explained that he was a traveler, newly-born among the lives of that land, and now the darkness found him both hungry and thirsty. He wondered if David would have some bread and some water which he might share. Without hesitating, David welcomed him. There, at his table, the stranger became Bernardo. David brought out bread, freshly made, and some wine as well — both of them simple and blessed by the land. Then, quite instinctively, and yet very conscious of what he did, David reached for the cup given him long ago by Athena. Into the cup David poured some wine. There, at his table, David broke the bread and shared the cup with the stranger. For the first time, David had drunk from the cup.

Once they had finished, kindness prompted David to invite his guest to spend the night, for it was already quite late, and that night the darkness had befriended the cold on its journey. Bernardo appreciated the invitation and, with a smile, spoke his gratitude.

With the morning sun came a new beginning for David. Without his realizing it, the promise held by the cup was about to turn into truth.

For David the past evening had been life-blessed, and thus he invited Bernardo to stay a bit longer if he wished — indeed, for as long as the spirit of either would allow. Bernardo heartily agreed, delighting in the invitation, for his years had been lived often in lonely silence, much like David's yet so many more in number.

The fullness of that first day was feasted upon by the two as they shared their pasts. It was then that David learned that his guest had only recently been released from a prison, though what it was that caused the imprisonment was never revealed. It made little difference to David, however, for to him the present and its seeds for the future were of more import than the fallow of one's past.

In some way, though neither David or Bernardo ever learned how, the fact of that imprisonment came to be known among the people of that land. While the villagers continued to be polite, they also began to grow distant. Not by intent did the villagers invite less frequently, not consciously did they share less of their comings and goings, but over the following months David found himself less a part of that community of inland dwellers. Had it not been for Bernardo's kindness and gentle presence, David would have found himself slowly returning to the loneliness he had left when he came to live among the people.

A year passed, and Bernardo one day told of his plans to leave David's welcome hospitality. The time had come for him to journey on, he explained. While there were a number of reasons — one being that Bernardo felt a need to plant and harvest a future of his own labors, the decision nevertheless painted a sadness upon those final days.

After Bernardo had left, David's former sense of loneliness again occasionally drifted through his day. At times, it would seem, it had even taken root. Once David had hoped that the people of the village would overcome their needless fear of a person who had been imprisoned, but that never occurred. Now David thought that perhaps the friendly acceptance of earlier days would reappear, yet that never came about either.

Outwardly, the villagers seemed unaware of the change that continued to take place. They went about their daily tasks, caring for their homes, tending their businesses, raising their families. Had anyone suggested to them that David in any way had been made less welcome, they would have protested. Yet David sensed that love was slowly becoming a kind respect.

Little had changed with the departure of Bernardo, though if the truth were really known, Bernardo had left with the specific hope that David and the villagers might once again share life fully. Yet it seemed that such would never come to be. There were moments when someone's kind word was taken to be new life sprouting — but that hope withered with the days that followed. There were smiles, but the joy was shallow. There were nods of good morning which never lasted beyond noon. The future, it seemed, could do no more than copy the past.

Many years went by and little changed. Once, perhaps a decade after Bernardo had taken his leave, David picked up the cup given to him long ago by Athena. He truly felt in need of meaning. His life certainly did seem lost. Finally David decided to drink from the cup a second time. Except for the villagers' change of mood when Bernardo arrived, life had varied little from when David had drunk from the cup the first time. He wondered if there would be any difference this time, or if the thought that the cup held a promise was again no more than a wish. Nevertheless, David did drink from the cup a second time.

Weeks after David had again drunk from the cup, a weary knock came upon his door from the heavy darkness outside. David opened the door to find Bernardo, in need as he had been once before. They embraced with joy and with tears. David quickly invited him in, immediately noticing that Bernardo had grown weak and sick. As they had done so many years before, the two again sat at David's table. Bread was broken and for the third time the cup was filled. Then Bernardo told his story of how he had struggled to shape his life in the years he had been gone. He recounted his few successes and more numerous failures, how all he had woven now seemed to be unraveling, and how this present illness, he had been told, would be his final struggle.

David listened — quietly, sadly, wishing he could offer strength. When Bernardo finished, David once again offered him his home. Bernardo hesitated. He knew in his heart the silent reason he had left years before, yet he was also fully aware that he had come hoping to find a resting place for his final days. So he quietly agreed and accepted once more the hospitality offered.

Word soon spread among the villagers that Bernardo had returned. What had been expressed in distant indifference ten years earlier now turned to harsh anger. No longer would the villagers quietly tolerate the presence of someone they perceived as evil because he had been once imprisoned. Now they spoke openly against him. When David explained that Bernardo had returned weak and ill, wishing only to pay life back with the last days she had given, only then did their resentment recede into a grudging silence.

During that month, David lived confused. He had drunk from the cup, yet he recognized no promise, much less any fulfillment. No longer did anyone smile, even out of politeness. There was no kindness, no interest, no care. It seemed as if all creation reflected the mood of the village, for the sun seemed less warm, the night heavier with darkness, the gardens less fruitful.

Despite all this, David continued to care for the aged Bernardo. As each day stole more of Bernardo's strength, so each day demanded that David share more of his. Within a week, Bernardo's world had shrunk to his bed. Soon David had to feed him and meet all his needs. Strangely, however, in spite of much weakness, the two would talk long into the night, sharing what each had learned of life and her people. In the end, the older Bernardo and the younger David reflected one another in thought as well as in holiness. Both suffered pain over the emptiness of the lives of those surrounding them. Both knew well that when lives are robbed of love, love is robbed of life, and the fruit of indifference becomes death. More than anything else, the enfleshment of this in the lives of the villagers caused them the deepest pain.

Throughout the month which followed, Bernardo grew continually weaker, and as that month neared its close, so did Bernardo's life. Later it seemed to David that Bernardo's passing had been an event of hope — dawn's light was born, the heavy darkness of night breathed her last, and Bernardo was freed for life. In the holy stillness of that moment, there was no more death.

When Bernardo died, David simply continued to sit beside the bed. There was peace — no sadness; holiness — no violence. In fact, little seemed changed. It was indeed a most unusual moment, for while David had grown alone in the midst of the destruction and alienation of those who surrounded him, he was not lonely. Having entered into the loss of one life, he had been gifted with new life.

III

In the ensuing weeks, David found it strange that once again the villagers were beginning to offer him welcome, even thought at times it seemed shallow. Most often it was a distant politeness or an obligated smile, but even those things seemed a monumental change from what had been. In his own heart, David found he resented what seemed to be the people's seasonal kindness. In the end, however, he decided he would allow the villagers to weave the future. While the days that followed never became an offspring of the joy which once was shared, a healing peace did begin to show signs of growth. Always David found himself wondering if the roots would hold. He was not sure he dared trust, yet he continued to remember that it was in risking to care for Bernardo that he had found life fully.

Then one wintry night, a knock on David's door shattered the frozen loneliness of his home. Opening the door, David stood looking into unknown eyes, both weary and aged. The woman who had knocked leaned into the open doorway, almost tottering into David's gaze. With a shiver, she asked if she might come in out of the winter. She wondered if she might have some water for her thirst and, if possible, a bit of bread as well. David paled. It was as if the cycle were to begin again. He wondered if his own spirit could survive another such journey, and yet he understood too well that to have closed the door would have been a greater, more final death.

David smiled, then, at the old woman who stood in his future and invited her to his table. Simply by the way she took her place, David knew that she appreciated his offer. He brought some bread and broke it open, as he had done once before, long ago. Then he reached for the cup, the same one from which he had first drunk with Bernardo. This time, however, his eye was caught by a design lightly carved inside its rim. Never before had he noticed the pattern. He looked closer, turning the cup in such a way that the inside of it caught the light. It was then he saw it to be not a design, but instead scripted words engraved into the cup and therefore into whatever it was the cup would hold. Reading the rim as he turned the cup, David's heart found the promise first made long ago:

Sometimes to be a ruined man is itself a vocation.

For a moment David's heart stopped. He found himself wondering if perhaps it would have been better had he never journeyed long ago into the woods in search of the one who is wise. He read the script one more time, afraid that he might understand more fully what he already knew in his heart. It was a strange moment, sewn with the thread of pain, sewn to a tat-tered past at one end and to an as yet unshrunk future on the other. It was a moment which might have lingered too long had David not placed the cup on the table, between himself and the old lady who had come as one more stranger. Between them stood the promise of his future. Into that future David poured some wine, and from the cup he then drank one more time.

Resonating Scripture: Mark 10:34-45

32

M. HELLMICH

A
STILLNESS
WITHOUT
SHADOWS

There is a promise made by the Faithful One to the woodland sprites and fairies of springtime. How the promise came about is a story for another time, but to know the promise itself is of great worth. To tell you, then, of that promise and how it touched my days are what I wish to share with you.

The promise is that in the springtime of each year, one day is always marked as the day of wisdom and truth. If one is sensitive to its coming and willing to journey the path it offers, it will always be a time of new wisdom and deepening truth to be held life-long. There is no one way to know its coming, except that by being aware of its possibility, when it does dawn, one simply realizes its presence.

I learned of that day, given in gift, when I was very young, perhaps eight or nine years old. While I watched for its coming each springtime, it was not until the spring of my 32nd year that I recognized it and its blessing. Though there has been a day so blessed every year since, it is that first day which has come to be special. This is how it came.

Trapped in our urban cobweb is a small, little-noticed river known as the Menomonee River by those who take the time to care. Portions of it have been allowed to live free, and those portions have been banked in gnarled trees and wild grasses and all sorts of green-time splashes. Indeed, it can be a holy place if one is open to entering into life.

On a morning dusted with late spring, I met a once-upon-a-long-ago friend named Michael, born on the edge of imagination with all the gifts of dreams. There we were, the two of us face to face — I, lying in the grass, chin resting on my folded arms, and Michael, standing tall and proud, all twelve inches of him. Though I have never been able to prove it, Michael has always insisted he is an angel, and to be honest, I suspect it to be true. We smiled at each other, Michael and I, the sort of smile which jumps up and down with excitement, the sort of smile which whispers "friend" and spins rainbows.

We sat together, there in the springtime sun, sharing wintertime tales of all we had journeyed since last we met. It was Michael who suddenly paused, looked into my eyes and said without hesitation,

Always the shadow, it is, which remains;
only the bird can cast it behind.
So too our spirits fly free of such chains,
leaving us as but shadows of another kind.

"Michael," I said in response, "why did you say that? What does it mean?"

"It is the answer to your wondering," came the reply. Then I remembered that Michael always knew what it was I wondered — he always said it was because he is an angel. To be honest, he did always know. Yet I still could not understand the meaning of what he said, and I told him so. Michael asked me, then, to explain what my daydreaming was about as he came my way that day.

"Well, Michael, there is this place of grassy sun, not far from here and along the river bank. It is where the path sneaks out from under the wild for no more than a flap of the river mallard's wings. Then the path slips back into the shadows of canopied summer coolness and winds on to copy the shape of the river. Just before I step into that brief clearing, I always notice it to be quiet and still. Always. Yet as soon as I make myself visible, the grasses swish, though there is no breeze. The saplings sway, yet there is no wind. The dried, stale grass of last year rustles, but no one moves. That always takes place in just the same way, whenever it is I come, but why it does so is what I do not understand."

Michael smiled, then. "Would you show me the place?" he asked. "Please?" And so the two of us made our way, past the children swimming in the pool of sun, over the bridge which joins the park not only to woods but also to wishes, and then along the path as it copies the river, deeper and deeper into what could be. We followed that path for as long as the stone riverwall continued. Where it ended, only a few steps remained before the path spilled out into the clearing. Both Michael and I stopped short. Standing in the shadowed path, the two of us slowly watched the sun-lit clearing. There was no movement. The grass stood silent, like thousands of flames which never flickered. There were no sounds — not the lazy heartbeat of the river, nor the groaning buzz of flies drunk with springtime. Michael and I stood silent and speechless, long enough for me to prove that the clearing, as we gazed upon it, was just as it would normally seem to be. Satisfied by the proof, I motioned to Michael, and together we boldly stepped into the clearing. Nothing changed. The silence remained — twinned by the stillness. I cleared my throat, as if to let the clearing know we had come. I said, "Hello!" and then quickly felt foolish. More silence followed. I walked back and forth with large quick steps, as if to scare whoever lived there into showing themselves. I sensed myself growing embarrassed, fearful that Michael would think me strange or confused or living in a world unreal. Desperate, I returned to the shadowed path and repeated my bold entrance, as if perhaps the first had gone unnoticed. Still — only silence and quiet. Finally I surrendered, both to Michael and to the clearing. "I'm sorry, Michael," I said. "It always moved before, whenever I came. It really did. I don't know why it didn't this time."

Michael only smiled and then, in a gentle sort of way, called me to sit beside him on the grass which lived there with the river. "Nothing's changed," said Michael. "All you said before is true, and what took place just now proves it so." I did not understand, and somehow my eyes must have told him so, for Michael paused briefly, looked at me, and then went on again:

Always the shadow, it is, which remains;
only the bird can cast it behind.
So too our spirits fly free of such chains,
leaving us as but shadows of another kind.

"The reason nothing stirred was because I was with you. You were not alone. When the grasses move and rustle, don't you know it's your spirit which is flying high, flying to the Faithful One? When next you come here alone and quiet, set your spirit free. Be still. Close your eyes, leave your shadow behind, and journey with your spirit."

I looked out toward the flowing river, back to the grass, and then to Michael, but he was no longer there. I was alone with the clearing — alone with the river and the grass and the silent sun. Then, as quickly as Michael had left, just as swiftly the grass began to sway, in narrow flowing patterns, as if the wind left footprints upon it. Again, as so many times before, there was no wind or breeze — only myself and the sun, now both silent. I remembered Michael's suggestion that I set my spirit free, that I close my eyes, leave my shadow behind, and journey with my spirit. What followed I cannot prove, but I know it to be true as sure as I know Michael himself.

With my eyes closed
and the shadow of my body behind,
I found myself —
or rather, my spirit found myself —
in an entirely new and different existence.
Though I could not see or hear,
by some new sense I was acutely aware
of all that was going on about me and within me.
In fact,
I was more aware of all that was taking place
than when I came to know through my ordinary bodily senses.

I discovered I was with all that surrounded me,
though my spirit was no more than a part of the one spirit.
Yet in some strange way I sensed that I was still me.
I was life — in the midst of life,
light — in the midst of light,
love immersed in love without a need to be loved.
I was a part of all the energy that flowed through everything,
and, while that energy did not begin within me,
neither did it exist without me.

I spoke with clouds
and walked with goodness as she sang her song.
I paused long enough to watch a game of tag
played between a whirl of greens and a flock of wishes.
The sunshine bowed as I slipped by,
and peace blushed as I stopped to kiss her hand.
I made friends with winter,
my long-time foe,

and was filled with wonder at discovering it possible
for a dandelion to be a rose.

In all that time,
while I was never more than me,
to have ever harmed or destroyed something other than me
would have touched me
and made me less.
In some real way
former limits had been overcome.
Though the shadow of my body had never moved,
nor had I journeyed within
as one does with insight or knowledge,
nevertheless, I sensed that I had traveled far.

When I returned, the clearing was again quiet, as it had been
when Michael and I had come. Something deep within me sensed
that I had journeyed far — and yet my body was no different than
before. In fact, I wondered how long I had sat there, cross-legged and
gazing. I was about to stand up, when I heard Michael's voice once
again:

Always the shadow, it is, which remains;
only the bird can cast it behind.
So too our spirits fly free of such chains,
leaving us as but shadows of another kind.

When I looked around me, Michael was not there. Only the river and
the sun and I remained — a trinity in the clearing.

I made my way home that day, aware of all creation as if it had
been newly made. Indeed — at least for me — it had been. The
promise had been kept. There was a day in the spring of each year
which was and ever would be a day of wisdom and truth. The Faithful
One is faithful and calls us daughters and sons.

LOVERS
AND
DANDELIONS

There are many stories of how the moon and sun became lovers, and I have no doubt that one of them is true. This, however, is the story of their parting, of their going and not their coming. It could have been different, I suppose, but then that could be said of all of life.

Among everything in creation, it seemed that moon and sun were the earliest of lovers. Some say it was because one was taken from the side of the other in the image of Adam and Eve. Their lives seemed to revolve in rhythm about each other as each reflected the other; and between the two there was disharmony which the rest of creation always respected.

The time came, however, when all of which had been created was to be put in order, each to be given a final task in cooperation with all else. Cloud was called upon to be the bearer of rain, and rain to be the bearer of life. Wind was asked to be the shaper, the one who carved the earth, smoothed it and polished it. People were sent among creation to be its lovers, keeping all in perfect harmony, but also being frightfully responsible for any harmony which their lack of love might cause. And so it was with all of creation; each was assigned a role.

Moon and sun were the last to come before the Divine Presence. Not only were they hurt and disappointed because someone other than themselves had been chosen to be lovers for creation, but now they were given roles which would separate them. Each was to be given charge over a portion of the day — moon over the darkness and

41

sun over the light. They protested, insisting others were more suited. But everyone knew it was the prospect of separation which the two feared most.

Nevertheless, the order of creation had been cast. In the end, moon reigned over the darkness and sun over the light. Out of gentle consideration for them both, moon was told she would be allowed on occasion into sun's daytime home. That is why it is possible to find moon's faint image in the daytime sky.

In spite of that gentle concession, sun suffered deeply over the loss of moon as lover. Wind tells the tale that early in their separation, sun retreated into the forest on a particularly cloudy day when his presence would not be missed. There sun wept large, sad tears for his beloved moon — tears which fell to earth, took root, and blossomed into miniature suns. The tale goes on to say that on dark nights, when moon was not in the sky, she was in the forest taking delight in sun's blossomed gift of dandelions.

In time, people discovered the forest carpeted with dandelions. Day after day they journeyed deep therein to marvel and delight in their new discovery. It did not take long before people decided to gather the forest dandelions and plant them in their gardens and around their homes. It was springtime, and all of creation was robed in a golden hue — the fruit of sun's pain and weeping.

Moon saw what was taking place, and at first was flattered that people should take such delight in the symbol of the love between her and the sun. Before long, however, she grew fearful that all the forest dandelions would be gathered and none would remain to mark her forest shrine. Therefore, during one dark night, moon made her way deep into the forest where she spent the entire night gathering all the dandelions which were present. When day came, the forest was barren of all the dandelions; not one remained. She, for whom all the tears had been shed, had gathered them and taken them with her to her home in the heavens.

As it once was, says wind, so it still is. Moon continues to shed a pale, yellow light, the result of being garbed in miniature suns, in fields of dandelions. Sun and moon still long to be lovers, meeting always on the edge of darkness and light. Dandelions are yet a springtime flower, announcing longer days and shorter nights. And the forest continues to grow lush, though barren of the tears that once made it holy for moon.

DAYNA'S
WILLOWS

At its close, this will have become a tale of the willows. For now, however, it is also the tale of Dayna, an elfin sprite who was born and lived for a time in the mountains of the north. When he was still young, Dayna had been caught unexpectedly in a late, winter blizzard, a storm which set him in search of a cave for protection from the wind and snow. By the time he had found such a cave, he had grown frantic, weak, and mercilessly lost.

Dayna's spirit survived the fear; and as both the snow and the cold faded, he found himself along the river he often viewed from his island village high on the mountain. That was long ago, and Dayna had decided then to stay by the river and make his home among the river's people.

He had been easily welcomed and quickly made to feel loved. At first, it was because he was so delightfully different from the river people. In so many ways he seemed to them much like the springtime which had brought him — spritely and light with life, short-statured and good natured, gently giving and never needing. In fact, there were some who named him "Spring." Though Dayna had never told them, he never quite liked the name, and perhaps that is why no more than a handful ever called him that.

Later, however, the river people discovered other gifts which Dayna freely brought and offered. They found that he always knew on which day the season would change. Oh, not the calendar date, for everyone knew that. No, he knew nature's day of change when the season would pass with the setting of that day's sun.

For example, Dayna knew the last day of winter by winter's last snow. And what struck the river people as strange was that he always knew which was the last snow as it took place. How could he know, they wondered, that there would not be another?

He knew the dying of spring, and thus the birth of summer, by the last flock of birds to return from the South, though what made the last flock different from the others no one understood. Summer was sealed, Dayna said, by the last day of the season warm enough for swimming. And autumn always faded into winter on the very last day of brilliant color, only to be proven by the next morning's winter grey. How Dayna knew there would not be one more warm, summer day or just a thread more autumn color — how it was that he could read the seasons — no one knew. No one but Dayna.

Also, Dayna could always tell if a love would last or not; whether it would bear fruit or whether it would wither and die. How he knew, no one could say. Yet he did know, and thus he became the village wise one.

Now, no on had ever asked Dayna how he could know the change of seasons or the fate of love. Nor did anyone ask, because no one thought he had the right to such knowledge. If the truth were known, however, Dayna would have shared his wisdom. But no one ever asked the question. It was as simple as that.

Dayna could have explained that he could not truly tell which love would grow and which would not. What he did know, however, was that if a love was born on the day the season changed, that love would endure. Why it would, he could not explain. He simply knew it would. Of loves born on other days, he knew some would last and others would not. Of these he never spoke. But the river people never noticed that. To them it seemed he had knowledge of every love.

So it was that the people who lived along the river grew to love Dayna, and Dayna them. Years passed, and both Dayna and the river people knew the time approached when Dayna and Death would meet in combat, one to inflict a mortal wound upon the other. Who, they wondered would then mark for them the passing of the seasons? More importantly, who would posses the wisdom to read their love? Though the river people grew increasingly anxious, Dayna's spirit remained calm and trusting. As he had grown in years, Dayna had also grown in wisdom.

One afternoon in late winter, when the stillness of that season was beginning to stir and grow restless for springtime, Dayna slipped away from the people and made his way to the bank of the river. He spent his time wandering, seeking a way to gift the river people who had been so good to him. Shortly before the day came to rest, Dayna discovered a growth of willow shoots, sleek and slender, awaiting life. There, in that lonely growth, Dayna went to each shoot and, with gentleness and hope, kissed it. As he did so, each willow came alive with blossoms of furry warmth. Then, as the setting sun sealed the day, Dayna returned to the village along the river.

That night Dayna gathered the river people and told them of a gift he had for them — a gift to last them all their days. During the final days of winter, they were to watch for the willow shoots to blossom, not with fragile color, but with furry warmth — hardy enough to survive the winter's cold. From that time on, the snow which followed the willow's blossoms would always be the final snow of the season, and also, therefore, the final winter day. Spring would always follow with the setting of the sun. With certainty, Dayna told them, they must know that any love born on that day would endure and bear fruit all its days. That is my gift, he said, to know the tides both of the seasons and of love.

With such a promise, the spirits of everyone rejoiced and celebrated the whole night long.

In the morning, the people realized that Dayna was not among them. They went to his home; it was unlocked, abandoned. They looked in the fields beyond; they were barren and untrodden. They looked to the mountains; they were snowbound. Finally, they made their way to the river. There they found the willows in bloom as Dayna had promised, each kissed with the hope which new love brings. In both directions, up river and down, far side and near, the river was guarded with sleek, slender willow spears, each furry and soft to the touch.

Later that week, the winter snows came one more time, bearing a white shroud for a dying season. Those who fell in love that day were blessed and quietly rejoiced. Out of that year's winter stillness, life was born, and in every year thereafter, the blooming willows heralded the end of one season and the birth of another, as well as a day when hope of love could be trusted and believed.

47

Thus, what began as the tale of Dayna and the river people among whom he lived, now ends as a tale of the willows. If it should happen, in the waning weeks of winter, that you come upon willows in bloom, give thanks and quietly await that season's final snow. And if, perchance, it is within your power to choose a day for giving birth to love, remember Dayna and the promise he gave with the blooming of the willows.

CHRYSANTHEMUMS

In his seedling years
he had heard those who were older
speak of God's word.
But when he asked what the word was which God spoke long ago
their words would stumble and trip
as they tried to explain.
Still, he kept asking,
hoping someone would tell him
what word it was
which God had once said.

One day
when he had asked his mother
one time more than she could endure,
out of exasperation, she finally agreed to tell him.
I think you are now old enough to know,
she explained,
as her eyes twinkled with a quiet smile.
The word God spoke long ago, she whispered,
was
chrysanthemums.
In awe he stood there before the revelation.
Chrysanthemums!
How powerful the word he thought.
How special it sounded.
The very fact that it was difficult
for him to even say
convinced him of its truth
and its importance.
Chrysanthemums!

From that day on
whenever anyone spoke of God's word,
he
along with his voice
would jump up and down
and shout
Chrysanthemums!
Chrysanthemums!

In time he grew old enough for school
and when the new teacher asked
what anyone knew about God,
he volunteered his wisdom.
Chrysanthemums! of course.
At first the teacher smiled and paused
pleasantly startled,
her imagination captured.
After a while, however,
the teacher grew more adult
and serious
for answers need to be correct and proper
and tell of how life truly is.
Chrysanthemums was not the looked for answer
he soon learned.

Thereafter
he was cautious
of sharing his bit of divine wisdom.
Oh, on one or two occasions
he had suggested chrysanthemums,
but others still seemed startled
and unable to understand,
trapped between laughter and confusion.
Yet his mother would not have lied,
he reasoned.
The truth must be in
chrysanthemums.

Years later,
when his wisdom had aged
like wine
and seasoned memories,
he came to understand
why only to a few in his life
had he entrusted
chrysanthemums.
They were those whom he loved
and
who loved him
with gentleness and with strength
like a flower

with long lasting faithfulness
and a common beauty
which survived the common.

Often he had daydreamed
why God would have spoken
chrysanthemums.
Why not a rose
or an eagle
or fire
or wind
or woman
or man?
Why chrysanthemums?
Truth, however,
is not always borne
with reasons —
more often with the heart.
And so he simply lived with his word,
absorbed its beauty
and became that word
enfleshed.

When he grew ill one final time
and memories gave the only strength that mattered,
he lay waiting
in silent peace.
A friend came, then,
one who had known his heart
and his dreams.
She brought him flowers,
chrysanthemums.
She placed them there on the table beside his bed,
and he simply smiled in thanksgiving
and quietly closed his eyes.

When next he saw again,
he found himself in God's presence
and this time God smiled
and said
Chrysanthemums!

THE
LADY
OF THE
GRAND

The Grand Avenue had all the signs of becoming Milwaukee's fairy godmother. It was as if she were capable of making every wish come true for those downtown merchants who lusted for the fruits of her magic. The Grand Avenue, you see, was the long promised healer of an economic cancer that had been slowly draining the wealth-blood of Milwaukee's downtown retail merchants. Now the new retail mall was to change all of that. It had been promised.

The new mall was wrapped in memories of old Milwaukee. Old fashioned brass railings and modern glass elevators together sculpted the inner space. Peddlers with push carts competed with multi-million dollar merchandisers as both seductively flirted with naive shoppers. The Plankinton Arcade, named for its founder who stood memorialized in green copper at its center, still remained the hub; but its consumer spokes now reached higher and stretched further than ever before. Contradictions abounded. Gourmet delicacies were available at fast-food counters. Designer creations stood side by side with racks of bargain basement specials in economically integrated aisles. Suburban commuters mingled with urban street people, both struggling to weave reality out of fantasies and dreams. Indeed, the Grand Avenue had all the signs of becoming Milwaukee's fairy god-mother.

The Grand Avenue opened with a flourish of trumpets and promises, and immediately the city responded to the call. She quickly became Milwaukee's economic mecca. Sometime later I decided I too would join the trek and form my own judgement of the city's new savior.

Slowly I roamed the layered mall, back and forth, level to level. The Grand Avenue was well named for she was both grand as well as an avenue of fashion, and I was taking it all in. It was so different than the suburban malls. All patterns of people were there - blacks and whites and orientals interlaced the aisles; both old and young found it a gathering place; high rise city dwellers and low rise suburbanites walked side by side with no rise street people. It could have been a taste of the kingdom if only they would have noticed or spoken.

As I walked the lower level I came upon a couple from the streets whose spirits were obviously lost. When I first saw them, I was yet a distance away. She seemed to be an older lady, hunched over and sitting on one of the mall's many resting places that had been gracefully placed beneath tall beautiful trees imprisoned in that artificial world. Standing at her shoulder and a bit behind was another, a gentleman with fewer years than she, though one whose youth had been lost years past. He simply stood there leaning over her and watching.

As I came closer the focus became more piercing. She who was seated was indeed lost — in so many ways. Obviously one of the street people, she wore an old tattered dress with her skirt pulled up above her knees and her knees spread far apart. As I came upon her, I noticed her to be drooling — not from the corners of her mouth, but with saliva that hung from her chin all the way to the floor. Her hair was greasy gray, stringy and straight and matted. Strangely, she wore an old winter coat, though the weather both inside the mall and outside was an early taste of springtime warmth.

With every step closer more was unfolded, for then I heard her moaning and saw her rocking — not as someone does who is sick, but rather as one who is lost, like a child, so frightened that she had completely retreated into herself trying to escape and deny all that surrounded her. I sensed I should help, but quickly anesthetized myself with the thought that she seemed not alone but with whomever it was who stood at her side. As I was about to pass, I noticed a mall security guard walking toward her. So it was, I thought, she would be taken care of.

Yet one more event seared my senses. As I walked by the three — the lady, her companion, and the security guard — I was burned by one of the strongest piercing odors I have ever come upon, stronger than decaying cancer or rancid urine or lingering death. I clearly sensed that if I were to touch her, I would surely find myself burned, scarred by the stench and marked with it myself. I quietly became thankful for the security guard who would take care of her and free me from my human responsibility.

I did walk on down the mall, but in doing so I had the strange sensation of having been cloaked with an opportunity to touch goodness that had been cast off. Yet I came to buy a pair of trousers, I told myself, and one should not be so easily swayed from such importance.

If that one moment had been my only one meeting with the lady of Grand Avenue, I believe my life would have gone on little different than when I came. Yet that chance meeting was not born alone. A twin experience was yet to find its way into my life.

For whatever reason, when I came to the end of the lower level, I decided I would make my way back by way of the outer sidewalk that followed the face of the stores and shops up Wisconsin Avenue. I had walked only a block or two. The avenue looked little different than before the mall. People still rushed to wherever. Curb to curb the street still overflowed with cars making their way from before to after. Here springtime still came in shades of building-gray. The avenue was no different. Then I suddenly saw her — again. It was the same old lady, now only abandoned and alone on the sidewalk outside.

The gentleman who had stood beside her inside was no longer with her. Gone too was the security guard. Only she stood there in springtime's twilight warmth. Looking up the avenue, her left shoulder was braced against the store front. To me she still looked lost — no more, no less than before. It did not seem, then, that there could be shades of being lost. She stood alone, moaning as before, still drooling from her chin to the sidewalk below, a gaze of darkness in her eyes. Most of all it was the smell that had not changed. No, rather I should say most of all it was I who had not changed for I walked by a second time.

This time as I walked on my spirit would not allow my mind to rest. My memory kept insisting on being noticed. "Thou shalt love thy neighbor as thyself." "I was hungry and you fed me, imprisoned and you came to visit." "God is love and whoever lives in love . . .", and on and on and on. I had indeed become a "professional God-man," week after week proclaiming how we were to live yet not living so myself. Finally I could go no further. I stopped and turned to go back, still not knowing what to do, or even if I would do. I simply decided to return.

My mind spun with questions. It seemed the police would certainly take care of her, wouldn't they? No one would ever be left abandoned in Milwaukee, I thought. What would I do with her? put her on a bus? but to where? She could not even talk or hear or seem to understand. She seemed so lost. In the end I concluded that the only thing that would make any difference was to touch her, to put my arm around her, to speak through myself and not simply with words. Yet it was the smell, the stench that I feared. I would be burned and scarred forever, I knew, if I would touch her. Then I too would smell as she did. That was what I feared most.

I continued to walk back toward her, still not knowing what I would do. As I came close, a stranger walked up to her with a hand out-stretched to her. He held a napkin, it seemed, or some tissue, reaching out to her as if to wipe her chin — yet not too close. He leaned forward rather than walking up close, and I wondered if he too was afraid of being burned by the stench. During all of this the lady never moved. She never saw the face nor the napkin held out. She did not push the stranger away, nor did she turn toward him, as if to welcome his gesture. She simply never moved.

The stranger, well, he missed her chin. Whether it was a fear of reaching into her world too deeply, or an awkwardness at being the lone human who showed care for another, I am not sure; but, with his arm extended, he walked up to her, missed her chin, and kept on walking by. He did glance back, as if to ask, "What now?" and in doing so his face looked confused. For a moment he became a woven picture of failure and love, of helplessness and of guilt. In the moment that followed, he turned and went on.

In a scenario that literally took no more than seconds and was totally surrounded by moving indifference, it now became my turn to do something, whatever that something would be. The lady was now no more than ten steps away. Briefly, I found myself angry — at her, for being a challenge to all that I believed; at the world, for allowing such as her to live lost and helpless; at the security guard, who put her out of the mall; at her companion, who had abandoned her; and ultimately at myself, for not being able to bring myself to help. In the end it was the stench that won. I too walked by for the third time — the last time.

More than anything else, for me one need remains — to find her so that I might ask her forgiveness.

Resonating Scripture:
Luke 22:54-62
John 21:15-18

PEBBLES
AT THE
WALL

To him it seemed that the wall had always been a part of the neighborhood. For as long as he could remember it had been there, like the picket fence his grandfather had built and the gooseberry bushes in the garden next door and Chippy the golden labrador two doors away. The wall had lived there as long as he — and probably longer.

When he was very young, the wall had been a place to go to play. Built into the river bank, it guarded the road from being stolen by the current of the river. Knee high above the bank, the wall had been set back from the road with its ends tied and buried in wooded green. There it had always stood, faithfully present.

In those years, the wall had been a good place from which to fish, for there the river was turned back into the woods with the current carving a deep pool at the wall's base. In those days, too, the wall had often served as a base camp for dangerous forays into the daydreamed jungle surrounding it. And on hot summer nights lightning bugs signaled across the darkness, sometimes to be caught to turn canning jars into lanterns, and at other times simply to dance a silent ballet upon a nighttime stage. Now as he sat on the wall, he remembered those younger days and thought them to be better— perhaps.

Later the wall had become a meeting place for him and his friends. "Meet you at the wall," they would say as they scattered home on bikes for supper and early homework. Then they would return, one by one, drawn by the call of the gang. Nothing much would ever happen then, except to be accepted by the others in the gang — something which he understood only years later. Once, someone sneaked out a can of beer, and everyone had taken a swallow as the dare had passed. Now, as he thought back on that, he smiled at how bold he had felt, and then how guilty as he slipped into the house and up to his room, pausing only long enough to let his mother know he was home. He had not wanted to get too close to her, lest she smell what he had been about. The wall lived with secrets, he thought, and never told.

Many times he had come to the wall, but only once in all of his grade school years had he come sadly and alone. That was when he was ten and his best friend was moving to another state. After the moving van had left and all the goodbyes had been waved, he made his way down to the wall. He remembered crying as he sat there, feeling as if he had said farewell to a lifetime. Indeed he had, as he now looked back, for every friendship in his life had been one of a kind — even the one that now brought him to the wall again, twenty years after he had been there last.

Now as he looked back, all of those alone times had begun as moments of sadness, much as this time — yet all had ended in peace. He thought of the time all of his friends had been invited to a party, everyone except him. Why he had not been invited he had not understood, and now it made little difference. What he remembered, as he sat at the wall, was the evening of the party and how he had come to the wall alone that night. Lonely and with nothing to do, he sat there for an hour then — maybe more — drifting in and out of feelings, angry for a time at being excluded, then vowing to get revenge, first at the one who had given the party and later at all those who had abandoned him to go. Then the anger returned. After a time, it gave way, and he was overcome by a heavy sense of feeling sorry for himself. Finally, spirit and heart together, he gave in, and he recalled the quiet sense of peace and calm that followed. It had seemed so strange, then, and he had not understood it, but in that moment all became good and nothing bad. There was no more need for revenge or hate, only now to stretch peace into tomorrow when everyone would be together again. Now, sitting on the wall, he saw it all so differently, though then it had been new and confusing. It had been a time of healing when the rest of life had been torn.

Alone at the wall, he moved through these moments one by one. The night before his graduation he had sat there, wondering what his future would be, feeling obligated to decide. That night the wall had been like a vantage point from which to view life as life's river coursed by. Another time had been occasioned by the end of his first love. She had told him, gently as he looked back on it, that the good times had ended. It had crushed him then, as falling into that love had crushed him earlier, similarly yet differently. The next day he had come to the wall once more, sitting and gathering memories in the midst of hurt and one by one, tossing them into the river from the handful of pebbles he held. It seemed to him, then, that everyone needed a wall in life, a relationship of love, a point of stability in life's flowing river.

Always he had gone home from the wall strangely at peace — never with problems solved, though always with them in place. It seemed to be the wall's gift.

Now he came alone to the wall again — in the middle of his life. A week ago his mother had phoned to tell him his father was very sick, about to die. He went to his father that night, and by the following morning his father had died. Funeral arrangements were made, and all the family gathered. Now his father had been buried, and everyone had returned to continuing life. Only he remained, to stay a few more days with his mother to help her sew a rough seam between two very different fabrics of life. Tomorrow he would return to his own life, but before he did so, he found himself at the wall one more time.

He had thought about the many times he had come before, and now his thoughts turned to his father. The memory of sitting on his father's lap as he read the evening newspaper drifted by and into the memory of sitting behind the wheel of the family car with his father beside him, teaching him how to drive. He remembered discussions over report cards and curfews and family responsibilities around the house. He remembered the time his mother was very sick and his father had cried. That his father was afraid had surprised him then, he remembered. Not now, however; he understood life differently here. He remembered, too, his father's scratchy beard when he decided not to shave for a day, and the sound of the family car in the driveway ˙ when he came home from work. He recalled the times his father had come to kiss him goodnight, even during high school, and the time he had left home to go to college when his mother and father had stood on the front porch waving goodbye as he drove off.

Tears quietly slipped down his cheeks as he recounted the many memories. With each one, he kissed a pebble and tossed it into the river, one by one, as he had done so many times before. He had always wondered why he had done so, and now more recently he wondered why it always seemed to help, why it was that the pain would slowly slip away.

Then, as he was about to leave the wall, he was filled with peace once more, and with life even as he lived with death. For some strange reason, he remembered what his father had said to him long before, "If you will be free, confess first that to which you are bound." So that was what the wall had always done — provided a quiet place for him to discover what it was that bound him. As he thought back, most often it had been a person, but also the past, and sometimes too his own need for what the future should be. All had bound him in one way or another — or he had allowed himself to be bound. And though they were not bad, indeed even good, they had been a kind of bondage. Yet, as he had come to recognize his bondage, he had always then left in peaceful freedom.

Like the wall which did not stop the river, but rather turned it back to the wooded lowlands so that it might find its way home, so death had come to his father, not to end his life, but to turn it back to the one who is Life that he might find his way home. In much the same way, he now understood, he had always come to the wall that he might be directed back into freedom and peace.

AN
APPENDIX
OF
STORYPRAYERS

GOLDEN APPLES

"Golden Apples" was originally used as a homily for a family Christmas Eucharist. As the story concluded, a soloist began the song "Mara," written for the story by a parishioner, Bill Callahan. As the song was sung, four high school youths carried a large Christmas tree down the center aisle. The tree was decorated with golden apples cut from gold poster board and trimmed with green paper leaves and was firmly set on a platform which the youths then carried on their shoulders, giving height and visibility to the tree.

When the song concluded, one member of each family was invited to come forward to receive a "golden apple." After all had returned to their places with an apple, the following comment and request was made:

Christmas is a time for joyfulness, and we who have come have been touched by that gift of joy and peace — much like Mara. The call of this feast, however, is not simply to find joy for ourselves, but rather to bring joy to another and, in that way, to give birth to Christ in today's world. Christmas is not about Jesus being born two thousand years ago, but about Jesus being born today. Therefore, I would like to offer you an invitation (or perhaps, more honestly, a request). Sometime today or tomorrow I would like to ask each family which has received a golden apple, to give that apple to someone else — to someone not in your immediate family and to someone who is not here tonight. Decide together as a family who that person will be. Tell them the story, and offer them the apple. In that way, you will give birth to the Lord Jesus through the joy you bring.

There were many disappointed sighs at the above direction, but many good things began to take place that Christmas. Families had to talk together about who the recipient would be, then go to visit that person. The story was told again and again. The focus of Christmas as present rather than past was reinforced. Stories about who had received the apple and how it had taken place floated around the parish for weeks after.

Mara

Bread That Remembers

This Eucharist was originally intended to be an all-school Holy Week celebration for the parish grade school. We did not want to celebrate the all-school Eucharist on Holy Thursday, since we understood that day to be a parish feast and wanted to encourage the children to join the parish with their parents on that day. At the same time, we did not want the all-school Eucharist to be one of the Holy Week feasts transformed to Monday, Tuesday, or Wednesday. The challenge was how to celebrate this week in a way which reflected the mood of the week without celebrating one of the feasts of the week.

When someone dies, the first thing we all do is begin telling stories of the person — insights and characteristics of them which we remember. Thus, it seemed appropriate and timely that, during this week, we tell stories of the Lord Jesus which we remember. This, then, became the focus of our celebration.

We wanted to create an atmosphere in which the children would feel free and comfortable to share the stories which they remembered of Jesus:

• It seemed that the church was too formal and too restricting because of the pews. We decided on the school gym.

• It seemed that the gym lights were too bright. We turned some off.

• It was thought that peers might make the students self-conscious and hesitant. We divided the entire school into groups of eight (one student from each grade level and appointed the two junior high students as leaders in each group).

• It seemed that chairs would distance people. We asked them to sit in circles on the floor.

• We thought forming groups of eight students, with one from each grade level, in the gym could be mass confusion. We created a school masterplan a week before and organized the movement into groups.

• It seemed that moving four hundred children at one time could be chaos. We played soft music throughout the school as the students came to the gym. (I have never heard the school so quiet.)

• We wanted the children to tell stories to one another (not to an adult who was leader), but we were concerned that without an adult it

66

might not get started. We scattered teachers and a few volunteer parents among the groups to overhear in case of "difficulties."

• Song sheets could be noisy and hymnals cumbersome. We taught simple refrains, able to be sung by memory.

The Celebration

The children, pre-assigned to groups, gather in the gym through the various doorways and seat themselves in circles at designated places. There is a gathering song, welcome, and prayer.

The Liturgy of the Word begins with a proclamation of scripture:

1 Corinthians 11:23-26

Ever since the time of Jesus people have shared bread and a cup as a way of remembering. For some reason there is something about bread that moves us to remember:

"Bread That Remembers."

The story does not end telling us whether or not the two brothers shared the bread and all that it remembered. Perhaps that is because the story never ends, because it always needs to be told, because people always need to share the bread and find goodness and find Jesus.

The days of Holy Week are days when the whole Church remembers Jesus. All week long, we tell the story of his suffering and dying and rising. It takes us a week to tell the story. But there are many other stories of Jesus to tell — stories of his birth, or of the good he brought, or of the healing and life he offered. Today I would like all of you, in your small groups, to tell stories of Jesus that you remember. Tell the story to one another and tell the entire story — not simply the title of the story or what it was about. *Tell the story.* Make sure each person in your group has an opportunity to tell a story he or she remembers.

Before you begin, however, some students will pass a piece of bread to each group — bread which we will gather later and use for our Eucharist. When one of the students comes to your group, take a piece of that bread and a napkin and place it on the floor in the center of your group. Then begin telling stories of Jesus, and the bread that always remembers will remember the stories you tell—stories of Jesus' love and forgiveness and healing.

(Allow 5-10 minutes for the telling of stories. When it seems that all have been given an opportunity to share their story of Jesus, proclaim the gospel.)

John 6:47-51

Prayers of intercession are then offered. Finally, those who distributed the bread are asked to gather it up again and bring it to the altar table. The Liturgy of the Eucharist follows.

*　　*　　*

The unleavened bread we used was made at the parish. Each piece was about the size that could be broken into 7-8 pieces. At communion time, the teachers distributed the Eucharistic bread to each group which then shared it with one another. Eucharistic cups were distributed in the same way. This eliminated the confusion of over 400 individuals coming to communion in a room which had no designated aisles for orderly procession.

A problem surfaced when we realized during the planning that the first and second graders would not be receiving communion. Having told stories to the bread that remembered, it seemed not right to prevent them from sharing in the bread. Yet there was a sensitivity that parents might not understand or approve. Our compromise was small crosses made of palm from the previous Sunday for each of the first and second graders. Indeed, the palm is a part of the entire story of Jesus as well, and they made those first and second graders feel special since they were the only ones who received them. They received the palm crosses from the teachers near each group while the others were sharing in the Eucharist.

The Golden Dove

This story originally received its inspiration from a story with a similar theme entitled *Sadako and the Thousand Paper Cranes* by Eleanor Coerr. For several pedagogical and liturgical reasons, it was decided to write a new story rather than to use the existing story of Sadako. Thus "The Golden Dove" came about.

This story is an advent storyprayer but could obviously be adapted and used at any time of the year.

The Celebration

The liturgy begins with a gathering song and welcome. A prayer unites us in the Lord. We are in God's presence.

The Liturgy of the Word

A reading from Scripture: Genesis 8:6a,8-12
The story: "The Golden Dove"
Proclamation of the Gospel: John 14:24b-28a,29.
Homily: This is the season of Advent, a time when we prepare to celebrate the birth of the Christ, the Prince of Peace. Yet Jesus will not be born again as a child this year. That took place 2000 years ago. This year he can only be born if we give birth to him in one another's lives. If we love and forgive and bring peace, then he will live.

This, therefore, is what I would like to invite you to do. When you return to your classrooms, your teachers will give you a list of peace projects. None of them is easy or simple. They all take a bit of time and work — that is how it is with peace. But for every action of peace that you do, I'd like to ask you to hang a paper dove from the ceiling in the corridors of school. Our goal is 1000 paper doves by Christmas. Perhaps then the golden dove of Christmas will appear in our school. Perhaps then when Christmas Day arrives, Christ, the Prince of peace, will have been born again in our world through you and me.

The Liturgy of the Eucharist follows.

* * *

The list of peace projects follows here. We deliberately did not include simple actions such as apologizing for pushing on the playground since we wanted to stress that peace takes some commitment. You are certainly invited to be creative and expand this list with your own suggestions.

1. Make Fridays during Advent "fasting for PEACE" days.
   - not listening to your favorite radio station or tapes
   - not eating between meals on Fridays
   - not eating desserts on Fridays
   - not complaining on Fridays

2. Work with a group of your classmates and develop Ten Commandments for PEACE in the classroom. Print these on tagboard and display in your classroom.

3. Make a WAR/PEACE collage. Cut out from daily newspapers articles and pictures which reflect violence, hatred, injustice, and also material dealing with peacemaking efforts, cooperation and correcting of injustices. Display in school or a store.

4. Write a definition of PEACE. Begin with "PEACE is . . ." Make it into a booklet with illustrations and share with your class.

5. Read the following Gospel passages which present Jesus' reactions to conflict situations: Matthew 5:21-24, 5:43-48, 12:15-21, 15:29-31; Luke 10:25-37, 18:15-25. Compare Jesus' words and behavior with your approach to PEACE.

6. Write a letter to the President, senators, representatives, or your local leaders and newspapers, making known your thoughts on PEACE. Share with your teacher and classmates.

7. Give up a candy bar, soda, etc. Put the money into a fund to send to hungry people. Sign your own pledge, set your own amount and when fulfilled, make your dove.

8. Compose a PEACE prayer for those who live in hunger or injustice. Say it with your family at mealtime for at least a week. Share it with your class.

9. Read a PEACE book and give a report to your class. Ask the school librarian for assistance.

10. Compose a word search with PEACEful words. Ask your teacher to make copies and give to your class or another class to do.

11. Keep a PEACE journal, a diary of daily efforts to be a PEACEful person.

12. Take one person per week in your class and be a friendly, spiritual, PEACEfilled "KristKindle."

13. Write a PEACE letter to someone you argued or fought with and apologize with them. Resolve to better your relationship.

14. Make a list of all the PEACE-loving things your parents do for you. Then write a letter to them and thank them for all these things. Send it by mail. What a nice PEACE surprise!

15. Write an essay on PEACE. For example:
PEACE is . . .
What PEACE means to me . . .
My hopes for PEACE in the world . . .

16. Interview people about PEACE and the arms race. Give a report on your findings.

17. Take photos of children around the school being PEACEmakers.

18. If you have any ideas for a PEACE practice in addition to the above, please consult with your teacher.

* * *

Origami doves proved to be too difficult for the younger children. We used a much simpler form of dove, cut from a paper plate.

We never reached 1000 paper doves. We did get to 492, however, and that was a marvelous achievement. Our corridors were filled with "flying doves." Some were skeptical of the junior high students. Wouldn't they be pulling them down? To the contrary, they were the most protective. Excerpts of their essays on peace were featured in the local newspaper.

Two additional dimensions might be incorporated. As the number of paper doves grew, one of the teachers added puzzle pieces of a huge golden dove on the wall outside the school office. In the center of the dove was a hole in the shape of a heart — peace is never complete unless we bring ourselves to the process.

An alternative is to have a papier-mache gold dove available. Any teacher who discovers a significant peace event in his/her classroom is able to request that the dove "appear" in his/her classroom — perhaps making its mysterious appearance while the students are at lunch or recess. During the next absent period, the gold dove then "disappears," but the work of peace has not gone unnoticed.

Step 1

Cut the paper plate as shown, and remove the shaded part.

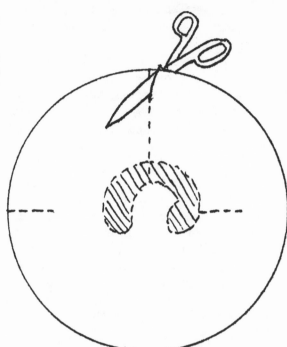

Step 2

Overlap wings.

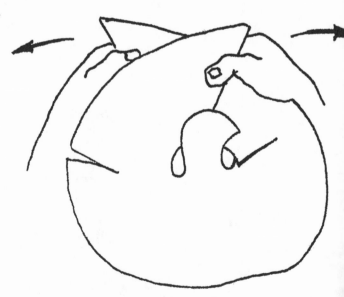

Step 3

Push the wings together by interlocking the slots

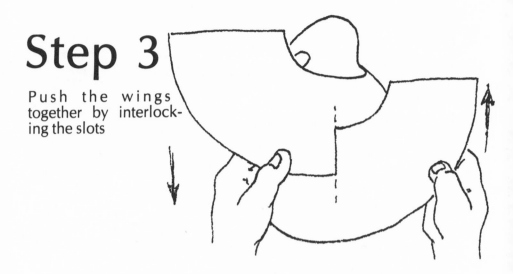

Step 4 The Dove

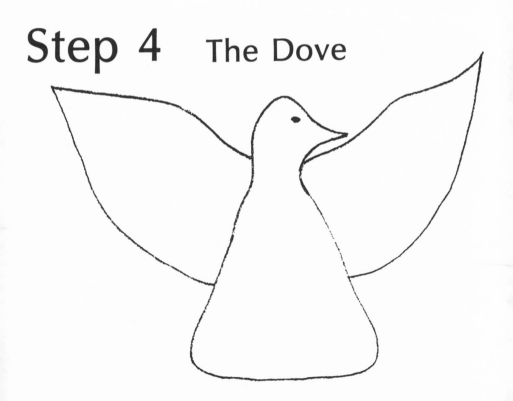

The Cup

Note: The inscription found inside the cup is a quote from the works of T.S. Eliot.

ORDER FORM

Use this form to order more story collections by Joseph J. Juknialis.

Send me:

_____ copies of **A Stillness Without Shadows** at $7.95 each.

_____ copies of **A Winter Dreams and Other Such Friendly Dragons** at $7.95 each.

_____ copies of **When God Began in the Middle** at $7.95 each.

_____ copies of **Angels to Wish By** at $7.95 each.

NAME _____

INSTITUTION _____

ADDRESS _____

CITY _____ ST _____ ZIP _____

☐ $ _____ payment enclosed (Check or money order; free postage and handling for all pre-paid orders; California residents, add 6% sales tax).

☐ Please bill me.

Charge my ☐ Visa ☐ MasterCard account

    Account # _____ - _____ - _____ - _____

    Signature _____

RETURN TO: Resource Publications, Inc., 160 E. Virginia St. # 290, San Jose, CA 95112.

XS